A Note to Parents

DK READERS is a compelling program for beginning readers, designed in conjunction with leading literacy experts, including Dr. Linda Gambrell, Distinguished Professor of Education at Clemson University. Dr. Gambrell has served as President of the National Reading Conference and the College Reading Association, and is President of the International Reading Association.

Beautiful illustrations and superb full-color photographs combine with engaging, easy-to-read stories to offer a fresh approach to each subject in the series. Each DK READER is guaranteed to capture a child's interest while developing his or her reading skills, general knowledge, and love of reading.

The five levels of DK READERS are aimed at different reading abilities, enabling you to choose the books that are exactly right for your child:

Pre-level 1: Learning to read
Level 1: Beginning to read
Level 2: Beginning to read alone
Level 3: Reading alone
Level 4: Proficient readers

The "normal" age at which a child begins to read can be anywhere from three to eight years old. Adult participation through the lower levels is very helpful for providing encouragement, discussing storylines, and sounding out unfamiliar words.

No matter which level you select, you can be sure that you are helping your child learn to read, then read to learn!

W9-CNU-689

LONDON, NEW YORK, MUNICH,
MELBOURNE, AND DELHI

Publisher Beth Sutinis
Editor Brian Saliba
Custom Publishing Director Mike Vacarro
Managing Art Director Michelle Baxter

Reading Consultant
Linda Gambrell, Ph.D.

Produced by
Shoreline Publishing Group LLC
President James Buckley, Jr.
Designer Tom Carling, carlingdesign.com

The Boy Scouts of America®, Cub Scouts®,
Boys' Life®, and rank insignia are registered
trademarks of the Boy Scouts of America.
Printed under license from the
Boy Scouts of America.

First American Edition, 2007
09 10 11 10 9 8 7 6 5 4 3 2
Published in the United States by DK Publishing
375 Hudson Street, New York, New York 10014

Copyright © 2007 Dorling Kindersley Limited

Published in Great Britain by Dorling Kindersley Limited

DK books are available at special discounts when purchased in bulk
for sales promotions, premiums, fund-raising, or educational use.
For details, contact:
DK Publishing Special Markets,
375 Hudson Street, New York, New York 10014
SpecialSales@dk.com

A catalog record for this book is available
from the Library of Congress.
ISBN: 978-0756-635107 (Paperback)
ISBN: 978-0756-635114 (Hardcover)

Printed and bound in China by L.Rex Printing Co.Ltd.

The publisher would like to thank the following for their kind
permission to reproduce their photographs:
(Key: a=above; b=below/bottom; c=center; l=left; r=right; t=top)
Dreamstime.com (photographers listed with page number): Tzooka 6, Phildate
13, David Coleman 16, Heinz Effner 21, Lee O'Dell 22, Philip Shaw 30, Johan63
32, Mmphotography 35, Ihor21 40, Rbbrdckybk 42; iStock: 4, 7, 14, 17, 23, 26,
36, 39, 41, 43, 44; Merlin D. Tuttle, Bat Conservation International: 9;
Photos.com: 24, 25, 33, 45. All other images © Dorling Kindersley Limited.
For more information see: www.dkimages.com

Discover more at
www.dk.com

Contents

DK READERS

Boys' Life SERIES

Night Creatures

Written by K. C. Kelley

DK Publishing

They come out at night!

When you're on a camping trip, do you wonder what is making that spooky sound in the night? As you lie in your sleeping bag in a dark forest, do you ever feel as if you're being watched? You and your friends might head off to sleep when the sun goes down. But a whole world of busy animals is just starting their "day" at work.

Animals that come out at night are "nocturnal." (Cool word time: Animals that are active mostly during daylight are "diurnal" [dye-UR-nuhl].) Not every animal can find its way around or locate food in the dark. Nocturnal animals have adapted, or changed, over time. These adaptations help the animals survive in the dark.

Buffy fish owl

4

This fennec fox has large ears to pull in night sounds.

Nocturnal animals depend on their excellent senses to help them find food in the dark. Most have very large eyes, which help them see well in low light. Their hearing is very good, too, many times sharper than a human's.

Some animals are predators and use those same senses to track other animals. Different animals use their senses in special ways that just wouldn't work as well during the loud, bright daytime.

Nocturnal animals also come in many sizes and shapes from giant bears to dog-sized foxes to tiny moths.

No matter what size they are, however, the creatures of the night each find their way through a dark and secret world.

Snap on your flashlight and let's explore!

Black bear

Look up! Bats!

Probably the most well-known night creatures are bats. In movies and stories, bats have become famous for swooping around the night sky. It's true in real life, too. Most bats,

Long-eared bat

all of which are flying mammals, are nocturnal. They rest during the day (yes, many do hang upside down!) and awake to fly out and feed at night.

Bats are very sensitive to light. During the day, they usually stay in shady places like caves or trees or under bridges. When the sun sets, they wake and feed, usually on insects. Bats are nature's pest controllers. Some can eat more than 500 bugs in an hour!

Austin's bats

In Austin, Texas, more than 1.5 million bats live under a bridge over Town Lake. Every night, people gather below the bridge to watch the bats fly out in huge swarms at sunset.

Scientists have named more than 1,000 species, or kinds, of bats. More than forty species live in North America. Among the smallest of those are the little brown bats, which are about as long as

Little brown bat

your finger. The largest are mastiff bats. Their wings spread out 18 inches (46 cm) wide in full flight. Most bats are about the size of mice or smaller.

All bats have some fur on their bodies. Their wings are made of skin with a single claw along the front edge. Bats also have two feet with claws that are used to hold on to their sleeping perch. Some bats also use their claws to grab fruit, small fish, or reptiles to eat.

Unlike many other nocturnal animals, bats do not have very good eyesight. In fact, have you heard the expression "as blind as a bat"? That comes from the bat's poor vision. So the question is, if bats can't see, how do they fly so fast and so well at night . . . in the dark? The answer is in their ears!

Bats depend on their amazing ears to find their way around. They use "echolocation." That means they hear the echo of their squeaks through their sensitive ears. As they fly, they send out sounds. Those sounds hit objects—a wall, a tree, a swarm of bugs—and bounce back as echoes. Bats have special hearing organs that let them figure out, from those echoes, exactly what's up ahead. Some bats can make a squeaking sound 200 times in a second!

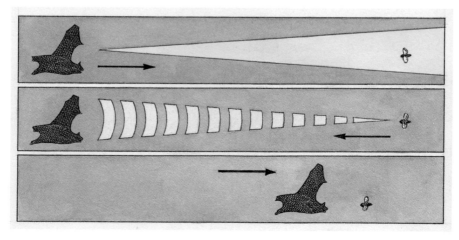

The yellow bars show how sound bounces back to bats.

Many bats also have very large ears to help them receive those echoes.

Echolocation works better when it's quiet. So bats rest during the day, when other noise would interfere with their echoes. They wait for the quiet night, when they soar through the air with the greatest of ease. Who needs light?

Fruit bat

Masks in the night

While bats rule the air, one of the most well-known night mammals on the ground is the raccoon. The circles of black and white fur around their eyes make them look like they're wearing a mask. They also have a very recognizable striped tail. Raccoons live in most parts of North America.

Along with a great sense of smell, raccoons have very sensitive paws. Their "fingers" are slim and very flexible. They use them to grab food and hold it while eating.

In the wild, raccoons often live near streams, ponds, or rivers. They are famous for often "washing" their food before eating it. Unlike many small mammals, raccoons are good swimmers.

Raccoons sometimes go out during the daylight hours. But they do most of their food-gathering at night. That banging noise you hear in the dark just might be a raccoon—with an eye on your trash! Because much of their forest

habitat is near where people live, raccoons have become very good at finding "people food." Most often, they knock over or  dig into trash cans in homes and parks. Remember those nimble paws? They're also good for popping open closed cans!

Raccoons will eat just about anything, from fruit and bread to leftover pizza. They have adapted well to life with people. Remember, although raccoons look friendly and cute, they are still wild animals and should be avoided.

Opossums are easily spotted by their pink noses.

Two other small mammals roam the nighttime world. Oposums are shy, quiet creatures who come out in the dark. Their large eyes take in all the available light and help them make their way around safely. Opossums like to hunt for scraps, much as raccoons do. Opossums also like fruit and insects. They are so shy, however, that when confronted by a possible enemy or predator, they simply lie down. They pretend to be dead. This is called "playing 'possum." Like raccoons, opossums have great senses of smell, too.

Another nocturnal animal uses smell, but in a very different way. Skunks waddle through the night knowing that they can meet any predator with a powerful blast from their scent glands. If you've ever smelled a skunk, you know why they can often walk around safe from danger!

Larger night mammals

Some larger mammals are not nocturnal by choice. Wolves and foxes, for instance, can hunt and move around during the daylight. However, so much of their habitat has been taken over by humans, the day is not as safe as it used to be. Gray wolves have been hunted so much, they are harder to spot than they used to be.

When hunting during the day, wolves travel in packs. One wolf is the "alpha," or lead wolf. He leads the pack in the search for big game. Wolves have an amazing sense of smell. A moose-paw track several days old can be enough to lead a wolf to its dinner (in this case, the moose). At night, wolves often hunt alone to make it easier to sneak up on prey.

Gray wolf

Foxes and coyotes are also often nocturnal. Foxes use their large ears to take in the faintest sounds.

One type of fox that lives in Africa, the fennec, has ears as big as the rest of its head!

Red fox

Foxes can be scavengers, which means they eat food that other animals have left behind. They might also eat the carcass of a dead animal. Being scavengers has helped them adapt well to living near people. Like raccoons, foxes don't mind helping themselves to a trash-can buffet. Unlike wolves, most foxes hunt alone.

Coyotes are comfortable at night, too. Their large eyes and good hearing let them track prey in the dark. They also have larger spaces in their head for smelling, letting them track prey easily by scent.

Coyotes are also well-known for their nighttime howling. If you ever hear their long, low cry in the still, desert night, they're just letting you—and other coyotes—know that they're around.

Coyote howling

Bears have several reasons for spending their nights out and their days resting. They're huge, for one thing, and can't exactly walk around without being seen during the day. Also, like wolves and coyotes, bears have lost much of their habitat to people. The closer bears

Black bears don't mind eating trash!

live to people, the less time they spend hunting for food in the daytime.

Black bears in the wild are night hunters, too. They use their excellent noses to sniff out berries and other treats. Bears can cover a large amount of ground during their nighttime hunts. Most species of bears return to their dens to rest during the day.

Most of these larger mammals are not adapted perfectly for the night, but they use their sharp senses to stay safe in the darkness.

Meows in the night

Nocturnal animals live with us, too. Housecats are especially active early in the morning and late in the evening. Our cats like to be with us, so they try to stay awake when we're awake. But they just can't help taking a long catnap in the afternoon. And they just can't help having a party at night.

Maybe you've heard your cat running around the house late at night, exploring the corners of your home. Or else you might have gotten up in the morning to find all the cat toys moved to different places in the house. Maybe your cat wakes you up at night to bring you a toy, or makes noise very early in the morning. She's not being a pest on purpose—it's just her nature.

Have you ever looked down a dark hallway and seen a pair of eyes shining back at you? Don't worry . . . it's just your cat (probably!). The eyes of cats (and dogs and a few other animals) reflect light in a special way that makes them glow in the dark.

Behind the retina, which is in the back of the eye, is a special part called the tapetum lucidum (TAP-eh-tum LOO-sid-um). Light that goes in the cat's eye bounces off this layer of cells to help the animal take in as much light as possible. When light from outside hits that layer, it makes the eyes shine.

Adaptations like this one help a cat find her way around when there is very little light.

Cats have two other super senses

that help them hunt at night. Their ears can hear the tiniest sounds and instantly figure out what direction they are coming from. And a cat can move its whiskers forward to feel as well as see anything that's right in front of it.

Housecats inherited their love of the night from their bigger cousins. The dark coloring of jaguars and panthers helps them roam the jungle unseen at

night. These big cats live in Central and South America. They can be as much as six feet (2 m) long.

Leopards rest during the heat of the day and hunt in the cool of night. The clouded leopard lives in Asia. It waits until night to sneak up on animals and sink his long fangs into the prey's neck. Leopards are great climbers and can strike from trees.

A lion's roar in the dark signals that the king of the jungle is on the prowl. Lions roar at night to communicate with other lions. The sound of their roaring can be heard five miles (8 km) away.

Leopard with prey

Mice try to hide amid leaves and sticks on the ground.

Tiny nocturnal mammals

One of the reasons larger mammals do well at night is thanks to smaller mammals. Why? Because smaller animals are midnight snacks for larger ones.

For many nocturnal hunters—from foxes to owls—mice are a key prey. Mice have to be nocturnal because there are even more predators during the day!

Mice search for seeds, fruits, berries, and other food on the ground. Their small size lets them hide amid the leaves and grasses. Their coloring also helps them blend in and hide from predators.

Even the mouse who gets in your house in search of food or shelter only comes out at night . . . when you, the two-footed predator, are asleep.

This gila monster finds a mousy midnight snack.

While you have probably seen mice, two other small, nighttime mammals are less well-known. Voles are mouse-like creatures who live in burrows in the ground. They are not very good climbers, so they don't go into houses very often. Like mice, they use the cover of night to come out from their burrows to search for food. They like to eat grass, bark, and sometimes snails!

Shrews are slightly smaller than mice or voles. They have long, pointed snouts, or noses, and use them to dig out insects, seeds, fruit, and more. They'll eat just about anything—shrews are almost always hungry. In fact, some kinds of shrews have

Meadow vole

The tiny shrew

to eat every couple of hours or they'll starve to death! These tiny animals are among the smallest mammals in the world. They don't only come out at night, but they have their best and safest success in the darkness.

Night fliers

The deep, hooting nighttime call of an owl is a cool part of almost any evening outdoor adventure. These awesome birds have adapted over the years to be perfect nighttime hunters.

One adaptation owls have made to safe nighttime living also works well *Eagle spotted owl* during the day. Owls' feather patterns match the tree leaves where they roost and sleep in daytime. Often you might hear an owl hooting right above

you. When you look up, however, you can't find it amid the branches. This camouflage also helps the owl remain undetected by the prey it seeks.

An owl's eyes are perfectly adapted to the night. Its eyes fill up half of its skull! However, an owl can't move its eyes from side to side as you can. To point its eyes in another direction, an owl has to turn its whole head on its neck. But what a turn— an owl can see almost directly behind it by turning its head around. The owl's enormous eyes let it take

Buffy fish owl

Bigger eyes

The owl might have large eyes, but they're not the biggest. The bush baby, a type of African loris, holds that record. This animal has the largest eyes, in relation to its body, of any animal.

in every bit of available moonlight. An owl needs very little light to see in the dark.

Owls hear very, very well, too. In some species of owl, you can see large tufts of feathers on their heads. The tufts look like ears, but they aren't. An owl's ears are just openings in the side of its heads, without external lobes. But those openings bring in all the sounds of the night so that the owl always knows what's going on.

Snowy owl

The owl uses all of its senses to hunt. Its sensitive ears hear the rustle of a mouse in the grass from many yards away. It pivots its amazing neck to focus its huge eyes on the target. Taking off from its perch in the tree, it flys almost silently. Its feathers are actually softer than other birds'. The owl's wings make no sound as the air rushes past the flying bird.

The wings power it forward in just a few flaps.

Out of the dark sky, the owl zooms in, eyes on the target. Its sharp claws reach out and snatch the mouse. Pow! The mouse doesn't know what hit it. One less mouse, and one more dinner for this great nocturnal hunter.

Great horned owl

Swamp bullfrog

Things that go chirp in the night

When you're out at night, it would be rare to see mammals such as wolves or bears. However, it would not be odd at all to *hear* other animals. But most of the noises that you hear at night are not made by mammals. There's the haunting hoot of the owl. It might be calling to a mate or its young.

Insects, birds, and even frogs make up the nighttime chorus.

Who else is out there? Crickets call during the day, but you can hear them better in the still night.

Many insects are active at night to enjoy the cooler temperatures. They can hide better in the dark, too, as they search for food. Their buzzes, clicks, and hums fill the night air with sound.

At night the deep boom of a bullfrog or the chirp-chirp of a green frog fill the empty spaces between owl hoots. It might be dark, but the nighttime world is a pretty loud place!

Cricket

Gypsy moth

Perhaps the most well-known nighttime insects are moths. Moths use their complicated antennae to pick up scents from great distances. Also, moths attracted to whatever light is around. Scientists don't truly know why moths flutter to the light so eagerly. They have several ideas, but no one knows for sure.

We do know that moths are just part of the busy nighttime world. Human beings are, for the most part, sound asleep as the moon lights the sky. Meanwhile, a huge host of amazing animals, adapted for the darkness, fill up the night with activity and sound.

Next time you're out camping, listen carefully . . . and know that you're *not* alone out there!

Find out more

Here are some other books you can enjoy to learn more about the habits and habitats of nocturnal animals.

Bats!
(Harper Collins, 2005)
Take a close-up look at the spookiest and most popular nocturnal animals. See more pictures of bats from around the world.

e.Encyclopedia: Animal
(DK Publishing, 2005)
A huge, photo-filled book that covers more than 2,000 animals and their habitats. Learn even more facts about the animals you met in *Night Creatures.*

Those Outrageous Owls
By Laura Wyatt
(Pineapple Press, 2006)
Learn more about just "hoo" these amazing animals are! The author answers dozens of questions about owls and their behavior.

Owls, Bats, Wolves, and Other Nocturnal Animals
By Kris Hirschmann
(Scholastic, 2003)
Along with some of the animals from *Night Creatures,* meet the lynx, the tarantula, and other nighttime beings.

Here are some Web sites that you can visit to learn even more:

Something for every boy
www.boyslife.org
The Web site of *Boys' Life* magazine is a great place to read about life in the outdoors—for both people and animals! New articles are posted all the time, so visit soon!

A world of animals
www.animaland.org
This site is run by the American Society for Prevention of Cruelty to Animals. You can read about all sorts of animals—even pets—that love the night.

Seeing in the dark
www.ebiomedia.com/gall/eyes/nocturnal.html
A science page that goes into great depth about the eyes of nocturnal animals.

Glossary

Adapted
Changed over time to create a better situation.

Camouflage
Coloring, shading, or patterns on skin, fur, or feathers that help make an animal hard to see in its natural habitat.

Conservation
Helping to preserve and prolong the life of a natural resource.

Diurnal
Being active during the daytime.

Extinction
The disappearance of a living species from the earth.

Habitat
The place or environment where a plant or animal normally makes its home.

Nocturnal
Being active during the nighttime.

Predator
An animal that hunts and eats other animals.

Prey
An animal that is usually stalked and captured by other animals who are predators.

Scavengers
Animals that eat dead animals or the leavings of other animals.

Tapetum lucidum
The interior part of an animal's eye that reflects light to create a nighttime "glow" effect.

Tissue
Any living part of an animal is made of this substance.